LEONARD COHEN
ANTHOLOGY

LEONARD COHEN
ANTHOLOGY

ISBN 0-8256-1238-1

HAL•LEONARD®
CORPORATION
7777 W. BLUEMOUND RD. P.O. BOX 13819 MILWAUKEE, WI 53213

Visit Hal Leonard Online at
www.halleonard.com

Bird On A Wire

Words and Music by Leonard Cohen

If I, if I have been un-kind,

I hope that you can just let it go by.

If I, if I have been un-true,

I hope you know it was nev-er to you. More like a

I saw a beg - gar lean - ing on his wood - en

crutch.

He said to me,

"You must not ask for so much."

And a pret - ty wom - an lean - ing in her dark - ened door,

Hey That's No Way To Say Goodbye

Words and Music by Leonard Cohen

I loved you in the morn-ing, our kiss-es deep and warm,___ Your hair up-on the pil-low like a sleep-y gold-en storm.___ Yes,___ man-y loved be-fore___ us, I

know that we are not new,_____ In cit - y and in for - est, they

smiled like me and you._____ But now it's come to dis-tanc - es and

both of us must try._____ Your eyes are soft with sor - row._____

Hey, that's_____ no way_____ to say_____ good-

bye.

Additional Lyrics

2. I'm not looking for another
   As I wander in my time.
   Walk me to the corner,
   Our steps will always rhyme.
   You know my love goes with you
   As your love stays with me,
   It's just the way it changes
   Like the shoreline and the sea.
   But let's not talk of love or chains
   And things we can't untie,
   Your eyes are soft with sorrow,
   Hey, that's no way to say goodbye.

3. I loved you in the morning,
   Our kisses deep and warm,
   Your hair upon the pillow,
   Like a sleepy golden storm.
   Yes, many loved before us,
   I know that we are not new,
   In city and in forest,
   They smiled like me and you.
   But let's not talk of love or chains
   And things we can't untie,
   Your eyes are soft with sorrow,
   Hey, that's no way to say goodbye.

Suzanne

WORDS AND MUSIC BY LEONARD COHEN

Additional Lyrics

2. And Jesus was a sailor
   When he walked upon the water,
   And he spent a long time watching
   From his lonely wooden tower.
   And when he knew for certain
   Only drowning men could see him,
   He said,"All men will be sailors then
   Until the sea shall free them."
   But he himself was broken,
   Long before the sky would open.
   Forsaken, almost human,
   He sank beneath your wisdom like a stone.
   And you want to travel with him,
   And you want to travel blind,
   And you think maybe you'll trust him,
   For he's touched your perfect body
         with his mind.

3. Now Suzanne takes your hand,
   And she leads you to the river.
   She is wearing rags and feathers
   From Salvation Army counters.
   And the sun pours down like honey
   On our lady of the harbour.
   And she shows you where to look
   Among the garbage and the flowers.
   There are heroes in the seaweed,
   There are children in the morning,
   They are leaning out for love,
   And they will lean that way forever.
   While Suzanne holds the mirror.
   And you want to travel with her,
   And you want to travel blind,
   And you know that you can trust her,
   For she's touched your perfect body
         with her mind.

Chelsea Hotel #2

Words and Music by Leonard Cohen

need you,   I don't need you,"   And

all of that jiv - ing a - round.

2. I re -   3. I don't

mean to sug - gest that I loved you the best, I can't

keep track of each fall - en rob - in. I re-

mem - ber you well in the Chel - sea Ho - tel, That's

all, I don't think of you that of - ten,

ritard.

Additional Lyrics

2. I remember you well in the Chelsea Hotel,
   You were famous, your heart was a legend.
   You told me again you preferred handsome men,
   But for me you would make an exception.
   And clenching your fist for the ones like us
   Who are oppressed by the figures of beauty,
   You fixed yourself, you said, "Well, never mind,
   We are ugly but we have the music."
   Chorus

3. I don't mean to suggest that I loved you the best,
   I can't keep track of each fallen robin.
   I remember you well in the Chelsea Hotel,
   That's all, I don't think of you that often.

So Long, Marianne

Words and Music by Leonard Cohen

Moderately slow, in 2

1. Come o - ver to the win - dow, my lit - tle dar - ling,

I'd like to try to read your

Additional Lyrics

2. Well, you know that I love to live with you,
   But you make me forget so very much.
   I forget to pray for the angel,
   And then the angels forget to pray for us.
   Chorus

3. We met when we were almost young,
   Deep in the green lilac park.
   You held on to me like I was a crucifix,
   As we went kneeling through the dark.
   Chorus

4. Your letters, they all say that you're beside me now.
   Then why do I feel alone?
   I'm standing on a ledge, and your fine spider web
   Is fastening my ankle to a stone.
   Chorus

5. For now I need your hidden love,
   I'm cold as a new razor blade.
   You left when I told you I was curious,
   I never said that I was brave.
   Chorus

6. Oh, you're really such a pretty one.
   I see you've gone and changed your name again,
   And just when I climbed this whole mountainside
   To wash my eyelids in the rain.
   Chorus

7. O your eyes, well, I forget your eyes,
   Your body's at home in every sea.
   How come you gave away your news to everyone,
   That you said was a secret for me?
   Chorus

Tower Of Song

Words and Music by Leonard Cohen

Moderately, with a steady beat

1. Well, my friends are gone and my hair is grey. I ache in the plac-es where I used to play. And I'm cra-zy for love,

I'll be speak-ing to you sweet-ly from a win-dow in the Tow-er of Song.

Additional Lyrics

2. I said to Hank Williams, "How lonely does it get?"
   Hank Williams hasn't answered yet.
   But I hear him coughing all night long,
   A hundred floors above me in the Tower of Song.

3. I was born like this, I had no choice.
   I was born with the gift of a golden voice.
   And twenty-seven angels from the Great Beyond,
   They tied me to this table right here in the Tower of Song.

4. So you can stick your little pins in that voodoo doll.
   I'm very sorry, baby, doesn't look like me at all.
   I'm standing by the window where the light is strong.
   They don't let a woman kill you, not in the Tower of Song.

5. Now you can say that I've grown bitter, but of this you may be sure:
   The rich have got their channels in the bedrooms of the poor.
   And there's a mighty judgment coming, but I may be wrong.
   You see, you hear these funny voices in the Tower of Song.

I'm Your Man

Words and Music by Leonard Cohen

Master Song

WORDS AND MUSIC BY LEONARD COHEN

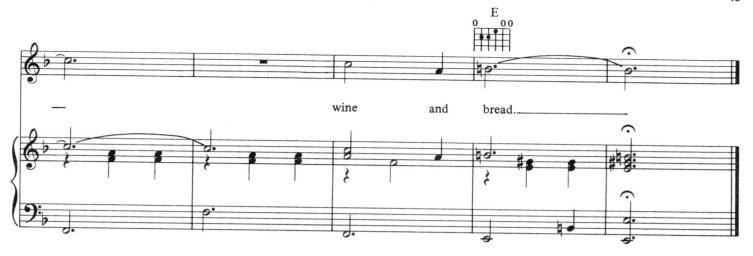

wine   and   bread._____

Additional Lyrics

2. You met him at some temple
Where they take your clothes at the door.
He was just a numberless man in a chair
Who had just come back from the war.
And you wrap up his tired face in your hair,
And he hands you the apple core.
Then he touches your lips, now so suddenly bare
Of all the kisses we put on sometime before.

3. And he gave you a German Shepherd to walk
With a collar of leather and nails.
And he never once made you explain or talk
About all of the little details,
Such as who had a worm and who had a rock,
And who had you through the mails.
Now your love is a secret all over the block,
And it never stops, not even
    when your master fails.

4. He took you up in his aeroplane
Which he flew without any hands.
And you cruised above the ribbons of rain
That drove the crowd from the stands.
Then he killed the lights in a lonely lane
Where an ape with angel glands,
Erased the final wisps of pain
With the music of rubber bands.

5. And now I hear your master sing,
You kneel for him to come.
His body is a golden string
That your body is hanging from.
His body is a golden string,
My body has grown numb.
O now you hear your master sing,
Your shirt is all undone.

6. And will you kneel beside this bed
That we polished so long ago,
Before your master chose instead
To make my bed of snow?
Your eyes are wild and your knuckles are red,
And you're speaking far too low.
I can't make out what your master said
Before he made you go.

7. And I think you're playing far too rough
For a lady who's been to the moon.
I've lain by this window long enough,
You get used to an empty room.
And your love is some dust
    in an old man's cuff
Who is tapping his foot to a tune.
And your thighs are a ruin,
    and you want too much,
Let's say you came back sometime too soon.

8. I loved your master perfectly,
I taught him all that he knew.
He was starving in some deep mystery
Like a man who is sure what is true.
And I sent you to him with my guarantee,
I could teach him something new.
And I taught him how you would long for me,
No matter what he said, no matter what you do.

9. I believe that you heard your master sing
While I was sick in bed.
I'm sure that he told you everything
I must keep locked away in my head.
Your master took you traveling,
Well, at least that's what you said.
I come back to bring
Your prisoner wine and bread.

The Window

Words and Music by Leonard Cohen

Additional Lyrics

2. And come forth from the cloud of unknowing,
 and kiss the cheek of the moon.
The new Jerusalem glowing,
 why tarry all night in the ruin?

And leave no word of discomfort,
 and leave no observer to mourn,
But climb on your tears and be silent
 like the rose on its ladder of thorns.
Chorus

3. Then lay your rose on the fire,
 the fire give up to the sun.
The sun give over to splendor
 in the arms of the High Holy One.

For the Holy One dreams of a letter,
 dreams of a letter's death.
Oh, bless the continuous stutter
 of the word being made into flesh.
Chorus

Jazz Police

Words and Music by Leonard Cohen and Jeff Fisher

Moderately, with a steady beat

Take This Longing

Words and Music by Leonard Cohen

1. Man-y men have loved the bells. You fas-tened to the rain. And ev-'ry-one who

all the use - less things my hands have done.

Let me see your beau - ty bro - ken down.

Like you would do for one you

love.

love.

Like you would do

for one you love.

Additional Lyrics

2. Your body like a searchlight,
   My poverty revealed.
   I would like to try your charity
   Until you cry, now you must try my greed.
   And everything depends upon
   How near you sleep to me.

Chorus: Just take this longing from my tongue,
   And all the lonely things my hands have done.
   Let me see your beauty broken down,
   Like you would do for one you love.

3. Hungry as an archway
   Through which the troops have passed.
   I stand in ruins behind you
   With your winter clothes, your broken saddle straps.
   I love to see you naked over there,
   Especially from the back.

Chorus: Ah, take this longing from my tongue,
   And all the useless things my hands have done.
   Untie for me your high blue gown,
   Like you would do for the one you love.

4. You're faithful to the better man,
   I'm afraid that he left.
   So let me judge your love affair
   In this very room where I have sentenced mine to death.
   I'll even wear these old laurel leaves
   That he's shaken from his head.

Chorus: Just take this longing from my tongue,
   And all the useless things my hands have done.
   Let me see your beauty broken down,
   Like you would do for one you love.
   Like you would do for one you love.

Is This What You Wanted

Words and Music by Leonard Cohen

Moderately, with a slight lilt

1. You were the prom-ise at dawn,— And
I was the morn - ing af - ter.
You were Je - sus Christ, my lord,— And

haunt - ed   By the ghost   of you and me?

haunt - ed   By the ghost   of you and me?

Additional Lyrics

2. You were Marlon Brando, I was Steve McQueen.
   You were K.Y. Jelly, I was Vaseline.
   You were The Father of Modern Medicine, I was Mr. Clean.
   You were The Whore and the Beast of Babylon.
   I was Rin Tin Tin.
   Chorus

3. You got old and wrinkled, I stayed seventeen.
   You lusted after so many, I lay here with one.
   You defied your solitude, I came through alone.
   You said you could never love me, I undid your gown.
   Chorus

The Stranger Song

Words and Music by Leonard Cohen

Additional Lyrics

2. And then sweeping up the jokers that
      he left behind,
   You find he did not leave you very much,
   Not even laughter.
   Like any dealer, he was watching for the card
      that is so high and wild,
   He'll never need to deal another.
   He was just some Joseph looking for a
      manger,
   He was just some Joseph looking for a
      manger.

3. And then leaning on your window sill,
   He'll say one day you caused his will
   To weaken with your love and warmth
      and shelter.
   And then taking from his wallet
      an old schedule of trains, he'll say,
   "I told you when I came I was a stranger,
   I told you when I came I was a stranger."

4. But now another stranger
   Seems to want to ignore his dreams,
   As though they were the burden of some other.
   O, you've seen that kind of man before,
   His golden arm dispatching cards.
   But now it's rusted from the elbow to
      the finger,
   Yes, he wants to trade the game he knows
      for shelter.

5. You hate to watch another tired man
      lay down his hand,
      Like he was giving up the holy game of poker.
   And while he talks his dreams to sleep,
   You notice there's a highway that is
      curling up like smoke above his shoulder,
   It's curling up like smoke above his shoulder.

6. You tell him to come in, sit down,
   But something makes you turn around.
   The door is open, you can't close your shelter.
   You try the handle of the road,
   It opens, do not be afraid.
   It's you, my love, you who are the stranger,
   It's you, my love, you who are the stranger.

7. Well, I've been waiting, I was sure
   We'd meet between the trains we're waiting for,
   I think it's time to board another.
   Please understand, I never had a secret chart
   To get me to the heart
   Of this or any other matter.
   When he talks like this,
      you don't know what he's after.
   When he speaks like this,
      you don't know what he's after.

8. Let's meet tomorrow, if you choose,
   Upon the shore, beneath the bridge
   That they are building on some endless river.
   Then he leaves the platform
   For the sleeping car that's warm, you realize
   He's only advertising one more shelter.
   And it comes to you, he never was a stranger.
   And you say, "O. K., the bridge or someplace later."

9. And then sweeping up the jokers that
      he left behind,
   You find he did not leave you very much,
   Not even laughter.
   Like any dealer, he was watching for the card
      that is so high and wild,
   He'll never need to deal another.
   He was just some Joseph looking for a
      manger,
   He was just some Joseph looking for a
      manger.

10. And then leaning on your window sill,
    He'll say one day you caused his will
    To weaken with your love and warmth
       and shelter
    And then taking from his wallet
       an old schedule of trains, he'll say,
    "I told you when I came I was a stranger,
    I told you when I came I was a stranger."

Humbled In Love

Words and Music by Leonard Cohen

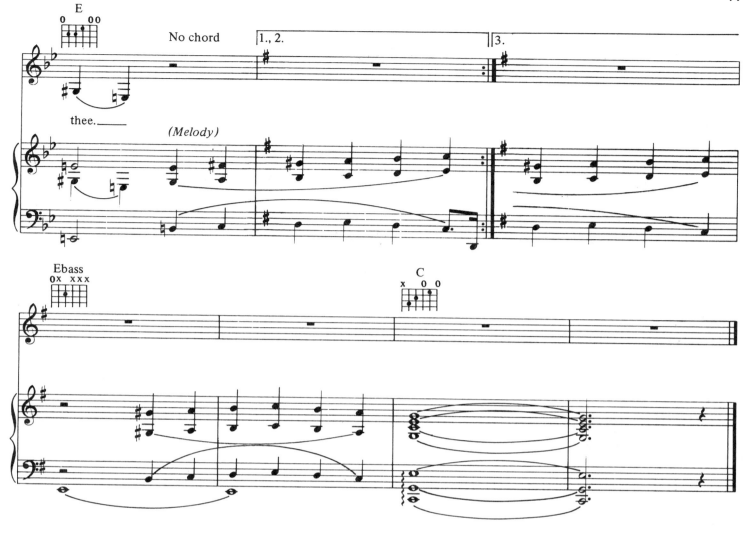

Additional Lyrics

2. Children have taken these pledges,
   they have ferried them out of the past,
Oh, beyond all the graves and the hedges
   where love must go hiding at last.

And here where there is no description,
   here in the moment at hand,
No sinner need rise up forgiven,
   no victim need limp to the stand.
Chorus

3. And look, dear heart, look at the virgin,
   look how she welcomes him into her gown.
Yes, and mark how the stranger's cold armor
   dissolves like a star falling down.

Why trade this vision for desire
   when you may have them both.
You will never see a man this naked,
   I will never hold a woman this close.
Chorus

Sisters Of Mercy

WORDS AND MUSIC BY LEONARD COHEN

1. Oh, the Sis - ters of Mer - cy, they are not de - par - ted or gone.

They were wait - ing for me when I thought that I

We weren't lov - ers like that, And be - sides, it would still be all right.

ritard.

Additional Lyrics

2. Yes, you who must leave everything
   That you cannot control,
   It begins with your family,
   But soon it comes round to your soul.
   Well, I've been where you're hanging,
   I think I can see how you're pinned.
   When you're not feeling holy,
   Your loneliness says that you've sinned.

3. They lay down beside me,
   I made my confession to them.
   They touched both my eyes,
   And I touched the dew on their hem.
   If your life is a leaf
   That the seasons tear off and condemn,
   They will bind you with love
   That is graceful and green as a stem.

4. When I left, they were sleeping,
   I hope you run into them soon.
   Don't turn on the lights,
   You can read their address by the moon.
   And you won't make me jealous
   If I hear that they sweetened your night.
   We weren't lovers like that,
   And besides, it would still be all right.
   We weren't lovers like that,
   And besides, it would still be all right.

Famous Blue Raincoat

Words and Music by Leonard Cohen

four in the morn - ing, the end of De - cem - ber,

D.S. % al Coda

3. And

Jane came by with a lock of your hair,

She said that you gave it to her ———— that

night that you planned to go clear.

Sin - cere - ly, L. Co - hen.

ritard.

Additional Lyrics

2. The last time we saw you, you looked so much older,
   Your famous blue raincoat was torn at the shoulder.
   You'd been to the station to meet ev'ry train,
   You came home without Lili Marlene.
   And you treated my woman to a flake of your life,
   And when she came back, she was nobody's wife.
Chorus: Well, I see you there with a rose in your teeth, one more thin gypsy thief.
   Well, I see Jane's away, she sends her regards.

3. And what can I tell you my brother, my killer,
   What can I possibly say?
   I guess that I miss you, I guess I forgive you,
   I'm glad you stood in my way.
   If you ever come by here for Jane or for me,
   Well, your enemy is sleeping and his woman is free.
Chorus: Yes, thanks for the trouble you took from her eyes.
   I thought it was there for good, so I never tried.

Coda: And Jane came by with a lock of your hair,
   She said that you gave it to her,
   That night that you planned to go clear.
   Sincerely, L. Cohen.

Ain't No Cure For Love

Words and Music by Leonard Cohen

I loved you for a long, long time, ___ I know this love is

(optional pattern)
(continued)

call to you, and I call___ to you, but I don't call soft e - nough.___

___ There ain't no cure, there ain't no cure, There

(as written) *(optional pattern)* *(continued)*

ain't no cure for love.___ *I walked in to this*

emp - ty church,___ I had no place else to go,___

(No) Diamonds In The Mine

Words and Music by Leonard Cohen

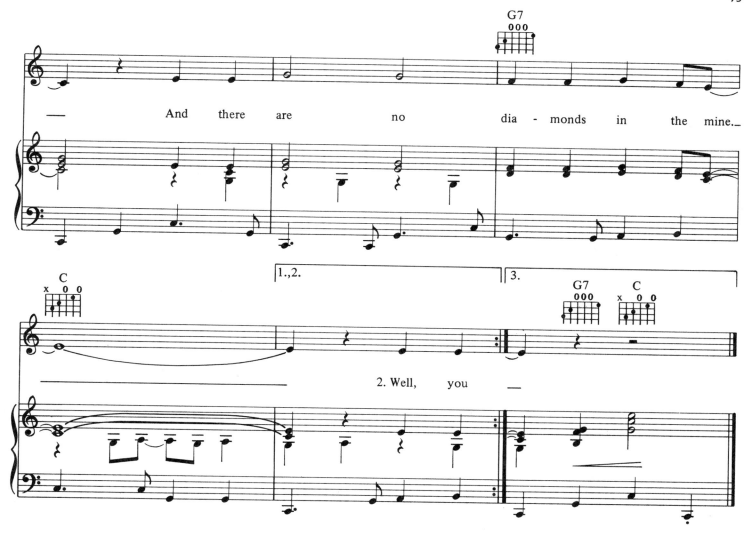

Additional Lyrics

2. Well, you tell me that your lover has a broken limb.
   You see, I'm kind-a restless now, and it's on account of him.
   Well, I saw the man in question, it was just the other night.
   He was eating up a lady where the lions and Christians fight.
   Chorus

3. Ah, there is no comfort in the covens of the witch.
   Some very clever doctor went and sterilized the bitch.
   And the only man of energy, yes, the revolution's pride.
   He trained a hundred women just to kill an unborn child.
   Chorus

STORY OF ISAAC

WORDS AND MUSIC BY LEONARD COHEN

moun - tain, I was run - ning, he was walk - ing, And his ax

was made of gold.

Additional Lyrics

2. The trees, they got much smaller,
   The lake a lady's mirror,
   We stopped to drink some wine.
   Then he threw the bottle over,
   Broke a minute later,
   And he put his hand on mine.
   Thought I saw an eagle,
   But it might have been a vulture,
   I never could decide.
   Then my father built an altar,
   He looked once behind his shoulder,
   He knew I would not hide.

3. You who build the altars now
   To sacrifice these children,
   You must not do it any more.
   A scheme is not a vision,
   And you never have been tempted
   By a demon or a god.
   You who stand above them now,
   Your hatchets blunt and bloody,
   You were not there before.
   When I lay upon a mountain,
   And my father's hand was trembling
   With the beauty of the word.

4. And if you call me brother now,
   Forgive me if I inquire
   Just according to whose plan?
   When it all comes down to dust,
   I will kill you if I must,
   I will help you if I can.
   When it all comes down to dust,
   I will help you if I must,
   I will kill you if I can.
   And mercy on our uniform,
   Man of peace or man of war,
   The peacock spreads his fan.

Tonight Will Be Fine

WORDS AND MUSIC BY LEONARD COHEN

1. Some-times I find I get to think-ing of the past. We swore to each oth-er then _____ our love would sure-ly last. You kept right on lov-ing,

fine, will be fine, will be fine, will be fine

for a - while.

1., 2. 3.

2. I

Additional Lyrics

2. I choose the rooms that I live in with care.
   The windows are small and the walls must be bare.
   There's only one bed and there's only one prayer.
   And I listen all night for your step on the stair.
   Chorus

3. Sometimes I see her undressing for me.
   She's the soft naked lady love meant her to be.
   And she's moving her body so brave and so free.
   If I've got to remember, that's a fine memory.
   Chorus

The Guests

WORDS AND MUSIC BY LEONARD COHEN

Chorus:

the brok-en heart - ed few. ____
"Let all my guests come in."}

And

no - one knows where the night is go - ing,

And

no - one knows why the wine is flow - ing.

Oh love, I need you, I need you, I need you, I

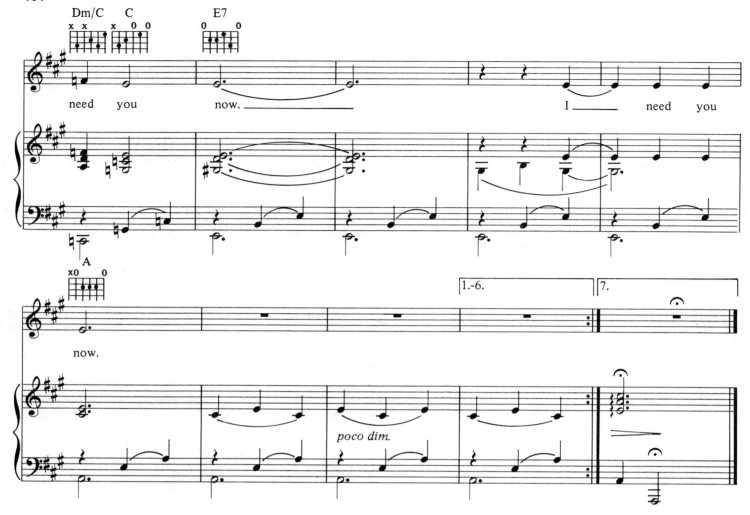

Additional Lyrics

3. And all go stumbling through that house in lonely secrecy,
Saying, "Do reveal yourself," or, "Why hast thou forsaken me?"
Chorus

4. All at once the torches flare, the inner door flies open.
One by one, they enter there in every style of passion.
Chorus

5. And here they take their sweet repast while house and grounds dissolve.
And one by one, the guests are cast beyond the garden walls.
Chorus

6. And those who dance begin to dance, those who weep begin.
And those who earnestly are lost, are lost and lost again.
Chorus

7. One by one, the guests arrive, the guests are coming through.
The broken-hearted many, the open-hearted few.

Sing Another Song, Boys

Words and Music by Leonard Cohen

Bridge I:

The mon-ey len-der's love-ly____ lit-tle daugh-ter,____ Ah,

she's eat-en, she's eat-en____ with de-sire.____

She spies him____ through the glass-es,____ from the

pawn-shops of her wick-ed fath-er.____

2. She finds him ly-ing_____ in a heap.
3. *See additional lyrics*

She wants to be_____ his wom-an.

He says,"Yes, I just might go to sleep. But kind - ly

leave, leave the fu - ture, leave it o - pen."

la   la.   La la la la la,   La   la la la   la la

repeat and fade

la   la   la la la la,   La   la la la   la la la la   la la la la.

Additional Lyrics

(*After 1st ending*)

Bridge II. He stands where it is steep,
    Ah, I guess he thinks that he's the very first one.
    His hands upon his leather belt now,
    Like it was the wheel of some big ocean liner.
    And she will learn to touch herself so well,
    As all the sails burn down like paper,
    And he has with the chain of his famous cigarillo.

3. They'll never, they'll never ever reach the moon,
    At least not the one that we're after.
    (*To 2nd ending*)

A Singer Must Die

Words and Music by Leonard Cohen

la,   la   la   la   la,   la   la   la

repeat and fade

la,   la,   la.   La

Additional Lyrics

2. And I thank you, I thank you for doing your duty,
   You keepers of Truth, you guardians of Beauty.
   Your vision is right, my vision is wrong,
   I'm sorry for smudging the air with my song.
       La la la la, la la la la la la,
       La la la la la, la la la la la la.

3. The night, it is thick, my defenses are hid
   In the clothes of a woman I would like to forgive,
   In the rings of her silk, in the hinge of her thighs,
   Where I have to go begging in beauty's disguise.
       Goodnight, goodnight, my night after night,
       My night after night after night after night.

4. I am so afraid that I listen to you,
   Your sunglassed protectors, they do that to you.
   It's their ways to detain, it's their ways to disgrace,
   Their knee in your balls and their fist in your face.
       Yes, and long live the state, by whoever it's made.
       Sir, I didn't see nothing, I was just getting home late.

THE GYPSY'S WIFE

WORDS AND MUSIC BY LEONARD COHEN

1. And where, where, where is my gyp-sy wife to-night?

I've heard all the wild re-ports, they can't be right.

But whose head is this she's danc - ing with on the

thresh - ing___ floor? Whose dark - ness deep - ens

in her___ arms a lit - tle___ more? And where,

where is my___ gyp - sy wife to - night?_

Where, where is my___ gyp - sy wife to - night?_

Additional Lyrics

2. Ah, the silver knives are flashing in the tired old café.
A ghost climbs on the table in a bridal negligee.
She says my body is the light, my body is the way.
I raise my arm against it all and I catch the bride's bouquet.
Chorus

3. Too early for the rainbow, too early for the dove.
These are the final days, this is the darkness, this is the flood.
And there is no man or woman can be touched.
But you who come between them will be judged.
Chorus

Seems So Long Ago, Nancy

Words and Music by Leonard Cohen

Additional Lyrics

2. It seems so long ago,
    none of us were strong.
  Nancy wore green stockings,
    and she slept with everyone.
  She never said she'd wait for us,
    although she was alone.
  I think she fell in love for us
    in nineteen sixty-one,
    in nineteen sixty-one.

3. It seems so long ago,
    Nancy was alone.
  A forty-five beside her head,
    an open telephone.
  We told her she was beautiful,
    we told her she was free.
  But none of us would meet her in
    the House of Mystery,
    the House of Mystery.

4. And now you look around you,
    see her everywhere.
  Many use her body,
    many comb her hair.
  And in the hollow of the night,
    when you are cold and numb,
  You hear her talking freely then,
    she's happy that you've come,
    she's happy that you've come.

Take This Waltz

Words by Leonard Cohen/Garcia Lorca
Music by Leonard Cohen

La la la,   La la la,

La la la,   La la la,

La la la,   La la la,

repeat and fade

La la la,   La la la.

Lady Midnight

Words and Music by Leonard Cohen

won me,   you've won me,   my lord."   "You've

won me,   you've won me,   my lord."   "Yes, you've

Repeat and fade

Additional Lyrics

2. Well, I argued all night like so many have before,
   Saying, "Whatever you give me, I seem to need so much more."
   Then she pointed at me where I kneeled on her floor.
   She said, "Don't try to use me or slyly refuse me,
   Just win me or lose me, it is this that the darkness is for."

3. I cried, "Oh, Lady Midnight, I fear that you grow old,
   Stars eat your body and the wind makes you cold."
   "If we cry now," she said, "It will just be ignored."
   So I walked through the morning, the sweet early morning.
   I could hear my lady calling, "You've won me, you've won me, my lord."
   "You've won me, you've won me, my lord."
   "Yes, you've won me, you've won me, my lord."

Love Calls You By Your Name

Words and Music by Leonard Cohen

Additional Lyrics

2. The women in your scrapbook
   Whom you still praise and blame,
   You say they chained you to your fingernails,
   And you climb the halls of fame.
   But here, right here,
   Between the peanuts and the cage,
   Between the darkness and the stage,
   Between the hour and the age,
   Once again, once again,
   Love calls you by your name.

3. Shouldering your loneliness
   Like a gun that you will not learn to aim,
   You stumble into this movie house,
   Then you climb, you climb into the frame.
   Yes, and here, right here,
   Between the moonlight and the lane,
   Between the tunnel and the train,
   Between the victim and his stain,
   Once again, once again,
   Love calls you by your name.

4. I leave the lady meditating
   On the very love which I, I do not wish to claim.
   I journeyed down the hundred steps,
   But the street is still the very same.
   And here, right here,
   Between the dancer and his cane,
   Between the sailboat and the drain,
   Between the newsreel and your tiny pain,
   Once again, once again,
   Love calls you by your name.

5. Where are you, Judy? Where are you, Ann?
   Where are the paths your heroes came?
   Wondering out loud as the bandage pulls away,
   Was I, was I only limping, was I really lame?
   Oh, here, come over here,
   Between the windmill and the grain,
   Between the sundial and the chain,
   Between the traitor and her pain,
   Once again, once again,
   Love calls you by your name.

Avalanche

Words and Music by Leonard Cohen

1. I stepped in-to an av-a-lanche,

it cov-ered up my soul.

When I am not this

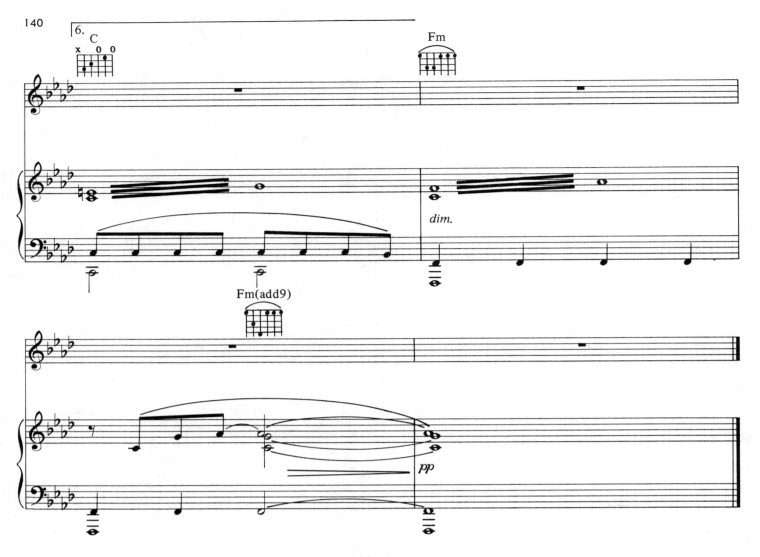

Additional Lyrics

2. You strike my side by accident
   as you go down for gold.
   The cripple here that you clothe and feed
   is neither starved nor cold.
   He does not ask for your company,
   not at the center, the center of the world.

3. When I am on a pedestal,
   you did not raise me there.
   Your laws do not compel me
   to kneel grotesque and bare.
   I myself am the pedestal
   for this ugly hump at which you stare.

4. You who wish to conquer pain,
   you must learn what makes me kind.
   The crumbs of love that you offer me,
   they're the crumbs I've left behind.
   Your pain is no credential here,
   it's just a shadow, shadow of my wound.

5. I have begun to long for you,
   I who have no creed.
   I have begun to ask for you,
   I who have no need.
   You say you've gone away from me,
   but I can feel you when you breathe.

6. Do not dress in those rags for me,
   I know you are not poor.
   And don't love me quite so fiercely now,
   when you know that you are not sure.
   It is your turn, beloved,
   it is your flesh that I wear.

Came So Far For Beauty

Words and Music by Leonard Cohen and John Lissauer

for such a _____ lone - ly choice.

And sure - ly she would ans - wer

to such a ver - y hope - less voice.

I prac - ticed on my saint - hood,

I changed my clothes _____ to black,

and where I would _____ sur - ren - der,

And now__ I would at - tack.

1. No chord

2. No chord

D.S. al Fine

2. I

I

Additional Lyrics

2. I stormed the old casino
   For the money and the flesh.
   And I myself decided
   What was rotten and what was fresh.

   And men to do my bidding,
   And broken bones to teach,
   The value of my pardon,
   The shadow of my reach.

   But no, I could not touch her
   With such a heavy hand.
   Her star beyond my order,
   Her nakedness unmanned.

   ℅ I came so far for beauty,
   I left so much behind,
   My patience and my family,
   My masterpiece unsigned.

You Know Who I Am

Words and Music by Leonard Cohen

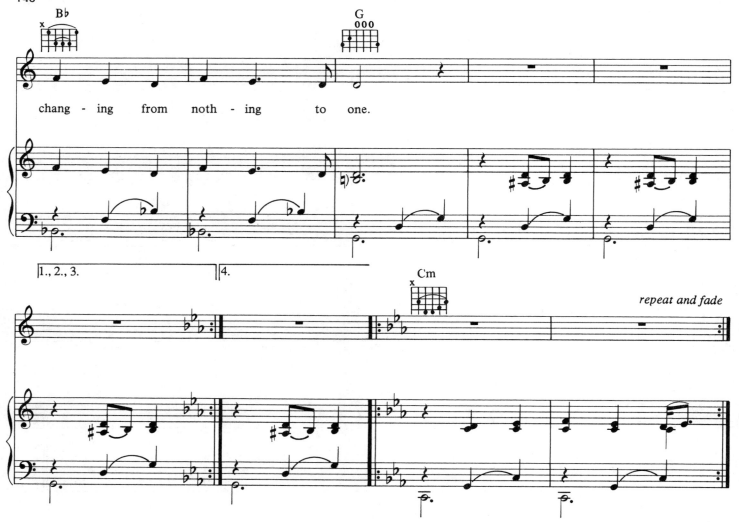

chang - ing   from   noth - ing   to   one.

repeat and fade

Additional Lyrics

2. Sometimes I need you naked,
   Sometimes I need you wild.
   I need you to carry my children in,
   And I need you to kill a child.
   Chorus

3. If you should ever track me down,
   I will surrender there.
   And I'll leave with you one broken man
   Whom I'll teach you to repair.
   Chorus

4. I cannot follow you, my love,
   You cannot follow me.
   I am the distance you put between
   All the moments that we will be.
   Chorus

The Smokey Life

Words and Music by Leonard Cohen

Additional Lyrics

2. So set your restless heart at ease,
Take a lesson from these autumn leaves.
They waste no time waiting for the snow.
Don't argue now or you'll be late,
There's nothing to investigate.
It's light enough, light enough to let it go.
Light enough to let it go.

Remember when the scenery started fading,
I held you till you learned to walk on air.
So don't look down, the ground is gone,
     there's no-one waving anyway,
The smokey life is practiced ev'rywhere.

Dress Rehearsal Rag

Words and Music by Leonard Cohen

2. **A** There's no hot water and the cold is running thin,
Well, what do you expect from the kind of places you've
been living in?

   B Don't drink from that cup, it's all caked up and cracked
along the rim,
That's not electric light, my friend, that is your
vision growing dim.

   C Cover up your face with soap, there, now you're Santa Claus,
And you got a gift for anyone who will give you his applause.

   D I thought you were a racing man, ah, but you couldn't take
the pace.
That's a funeral in the mirror, and it's stopping at your face.

   E That's right, it's come to this.
Yes, it's come to this,
And wasn't it a long way down?
Ah, wasn't it a strange way down?

3. **A** Once there was a path and girl with chestnut hair,
And you passed the summers picking all of the berries that
grew there.

   B There were times she was a woman, there were times she was
just a child,
And you held her in the shadows where the raspberries grow wild.

   C And you climbed the twilight mountains, and you sang about the
view,
And ev'rywhere you wandered, love seemed to go along with you.

   D That's a hard one to remember, yes, it makes you clench your fist,
And the veins stand out like highways all along your wrist.

   E And yes, it's come to this.
It's come to this,
And wasn't it a long way down?
And wasn't it a strange way down?

4. **A** You can still find a job, go out and talk to a friend,
On the back of every magazine, there are those coupons you
can sand.

   B Why don't you join the Rosicrucians? They will give you
back your hope,
You can find your love with diagrams on a plain brown
envelope.

   C But you've used up all coupons, except the one that seems
To be written on your wrist along with several thousand
dreams.

   D Now Santa Claus comes forward, that's a razor in his mitt,
And he puts on his dark glasses, and he
shows you where to hit.

   E And then the cameras pan, the stand-in stunt man,
dress rehearsal rag.
It's just the dress rehearsal rag,
You know this dress reharsal rag,
It's just the dress rehearsal rag.

There Is A War

Words and Music by Leonard Cohen

4. There is a war be - tween the rich and poor, a

war be - tween the man and the wom - an. There is a

war be - tween the left and right, a war be - tween the black and white, a

war be - tween the odd and the e - ven. Why don't you

Joan Of Arc

Words and Music by Leonard Cohen

la.

Additional Lyrics

2. Well, I'm glad to hear you talk this way,
   You know I've watched you riding ev'ry day.
   Something in me yearns to win
   Such a cold and lonesome heroine.
   "And who are you," she sternly spoke
   To the one beneath the smoke.
   "Why I'm fire," he replied,
   "And I love your solitude, I love your pride."
   Chorus

3. "Then fire make your body cold,
   I'm gonna give you mine to hold."
   Saying this, she climbed inside
   To be his one, to be his only bride.
   And deep into his fiery heart,
   He took the dust of Joan of Arc.
   And high above the wedding guests,
   He hung the ashes of her wedding dress.
   Chorus

4. It was deep into his fiery heart
   He took the dust of Joan of Arc.
   And then she clearly understood,
   If he was fire, oh, then she must be wood.
   I saw her wince, I saw her cry,
   I saw the glory in her eye.
   Myself, I long for love and light,
   But must it come so cruel and, oh, so bright!
   Chorus

Winter Lady

Words and Music by Leonard Cohen

when I___ was a sol - dier, And I___

___ fought ev - 'ry___ man for her___ un -

til the nights grew cold - er.

Additional Lyrics

2. She used to wear her hair like you,
Except when she was sleeping.
And then she'd weave it on a loom
Of smoke and gold and breathing.
  And why are you so quiet now,
  Standing there in the doorway?
  You chose your journey long before
  You came upon this highway.

Trav'ling lady, stay awhile
Until the night is over.
I'm just a station on your way,
I know I'm not your lover.

One Of Us Cannot Be Wrong

Words and Music by Leonard Cohen

Additional Lyrics

2. I showed my heart to the doctor,
   He said I'd just have to quit.
   Then he wrote himself a prescription,
   And your name was mentioned in it.
   Then he locked himself in a library shelf
   With the details of our honeymoon.
   And I hear from the nurse
   That he's gotten much worse,
   And his practice is all in a ruin.

3. I heard of a saint who had loved you,
   I studied all night in his school.
   He taught that the duty of lovers
   Is to tarnish the golden rule.
   And just when I was sure
   That his teachings were pure,
   He drowned himself in the pool.
   His body is gone, but back here on the lawn,
   His spirit continues to drool.

4. An Eskimo showed me a movie
   He'd recently taken of you.
   The poor man could hardly stop shivering,
   His lips and his fingers were blue.
   I suppose that he froze
   When the wind took your clothes,
   And I guess he just never got warm.
   But you stand there so nice in your blizzard of ice,
   O, please let me come into the storm.

Why Don't You Try

WORDS AND MUSIC BY LEONARD COHEN

own.　　　　　　　　　　2. Why　don't　you

Additional Lyrics

2. Why don't you try to forget him,
   Just open up your dainty little hand.
   You know this life is filled with many sweet companions,
   Many satisfying one-night stands.

   Do you want to be the ditch around the tower?
   Do you want to be the moonlight in his cave?
   Do you want to give your blessing to his power
   As he goes whistling past his daddy, past his daddy's grave?

3. I'd like to take you to the ceremony,
   Well, that is if I remember the way.
   You see Jack and Jill, they're gonna join their misery,
   And I'm afraid it's time for everyone to pray.

   You can see they've finally taken cover,
   They're willing, yeah, they're willing to obey.
   Their vows are difficult, they're for each other,
   So let nobody put a loophole, a loophole in their way.

THE TRAITOR

WORDS AND MUSIC BY LEONARD COHEN

1. Now the swan, it float-ed on the Eng-lish riv-er.

Ah, the rose of high ro-mance, it o-pened

wide. A sun-tanned wom-an

Additional Lyrics

4. The judges said, "You missed it by a fraction,
   Rise up and brace your troops for the attack.
   The dreamers ride against the men of action,
   Oh, see the men of action falling back."

5. But I lingered on her thighs a fatal moment,
   I kissed her lips as though I thirsted still.
   My falsity, it stung me like a hornet,
   The poison sank and it paralysed my will.

6. I could not move to warn the younger soldiers
   That they had been deserted from above.
   So on battlefields from here to Barcelona,
   I'm listed with the enemies of love.

7. And long ago she said, "I must be leaving,
   But keep my body here to lie upon.
   You can move it up and down and when I'm sleeping,
   Run some wire through that rose and wind the swan."

8. So daily I renew my idle duty,
   I touch her here and there, I know my place.
   I kiss her open mouth and I praise her beauty,
   And people call me "Traitor" to my face.

Who By Fire

WORDS AND MUSIC BY LEONARD COHEN

ing?

2. And

repeat and fade

Additional Lyrics

2. And who in her lonely slip,
   Who by barbiturate?
   Who in these realms of love,
   Who by something blunt?
   Who by avalanche,
   Who by powder?
   Who for his greed,
   Who for his hunger?
   And who shall I say is calling?

3. And who by brave ascent,
   Who by accident?
   Who in solitude,
   Who in this mirror?
   Who by his lady's command,
   Who by his own hand?
   Who in mortal chains,
   Who in power?
   And who shall I say is calling?

First We Take Manhattan

Words and Music by Leonard Cohen

I'd real - ly like to live be - side —— you,

ba - by.—— I love your bod - y and your

spir - it and your clothes. But you

see that line there mov - ing through the sta - tion? ——

Additional Lyrics

From D.S.
I don't like your fashion business, mister.
I don't like these drugs that keep you thin.
I don't like what happened to my sister.
First we take Manhattan, then we take Berlin.

(Bridge):
I'd really like to live beside you, baby.
I love your body and your spirit and your clothes.
But you see that line there moving through the station?
And I told you, and I told you,
I told you I was one of those,

And I thank you for those items that you sent me:
The monkey and the plywood violin.
I practiced every night and now I'm ready.
First we take Manhattan, then we take Berlin. *(To Coda)*

Everybody Knows

WORDS AND MUSIC BY LEONARD COHEN AND SHARON ROBINSON

knows that the boat is leak - ing. Ev - ery - bod - y

knows the cap - tain lied. Ev - ery - bod - y got this brok - en

feel - ing like their fa - ther or their dog just died.

Ev - ery - bod - y talk - ing to their pock - ets. Ev - ery - bod - y

knows.　　　　　　　Ev-ery-bod-y knows.　　　　　That's　　how it

goes.　　　　　Oh,　　ev-ery-bod-y　knows. _____

Additional Lyrics

4. And everybody knows that it's now or never.
Everybody knows that it's me or you.
And everybody knows that you live forever
When you've done a line or two.
Everybody knows the deal is rotten:
Old Black Joe's still pickin' cotton
For your ribbons and bows. And everybody knows.

5. Everybody knows that the plague is coming.
Everybody knows thats it's moving fast.
Everybody knows that the naked man and woman
Are just a shining artifact of the past.
Everybody knows the scene is dead,
But there's gonna be a meter on your bed
That will disclose what everybody knows.

6. And everybody knows that you're in trouble.
Everybody knows what you've been through,
From the bloody cross on top of Calvary
To the beach of Malibu.
Everybody knows it's coming apart:
Take one last look at this Sacred Heart
Before it blows. And everybody knows.

Lover Lover Lover

Words and Music by Leonard Cohen

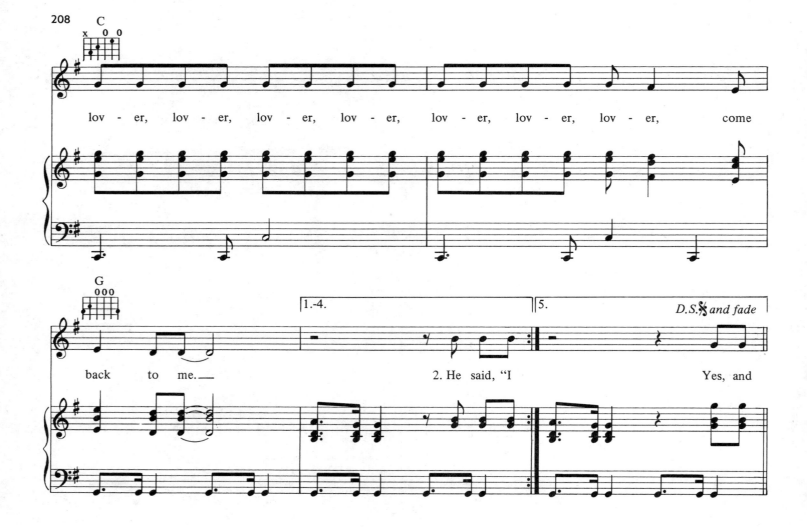

lov - er, lov - er, lov - er, lov - er, lov - er, lov - er, lov - er, come

back to me. ___ 2. He said, "I Yes, and

Additional Lyrics

2. He said, "I locked you in this body, I meant it as a kind of trial.
You can use it for a weapon or to make some woman smile."
Chorus

3. "Then let me start again,"I cried,"Please let me start again.
I want a face that's fair this time. I want a spirit that is calm."
Chorus

4. "I never turned aside,"he said," I never walked away.
It was you who built the temple, it was you who covered up my face."
Chorus

5. And may the spirit of this song, may it rise up pure and free.
May it be a shield for you, a shield against the enemy.
Chorus and fade